On the M

GW01072059

On the Move in a Gypsy Waggon

Published by Robert Dawson, 2007
188 Alfreton Road,
Blackwell,
Alfreton,
Derbys.
DE55 5JH

ISBN 978-1-903418-36-9

Printed by 4 Sheets Design and Print
197 Mansfield Road, Nottingham, NG1 3FS

Introduction

It is my hope that this little book will be an interesting insight for those that have never been introduced to a Gypsy Waggon before.

There are many fine waggons to be seen around the country and I hope having read this, your curiosity will be aroused. There are also definitive works on the subject by other authors and much can be learned from seeking them out also.

I would like to thank my friends Diane and Andrew Mott for their help with the typing and the use of their computer, as well as Bob Dawson. I hope you will enjoy the fruits of our labours.

And yes, we do know waggon usually has only one 'g' — but if its good enough for Dennis Harvey, John Thompson, Barrie Law and my dad!...

Ryalla Duffy

This book is dedicated to Keith Smith, shown here with my son Joeboy: the gry being George Washington.

Keith often travelled with us.

Keith died on 24th March 2007.

A true Rye

The Waggon

When Gypsies first travelled in this country, it was with pack ponies to carry the rods and sheets for their tents. As the Gypsies became richer and roadways improved, carts were used. At first, rods were bent over the top of the carts and a rough accommodation top made by covering the rods with sheets. From this, evolved the first Gypsy living waggons. The Romany word is *Vardo* and affectionately they are also known as bow-tops or barrel-tops if they are not of the Ledge or Showman's type. We still live and travel in a bow-top waggon so I'm going to tell you about them first

By the mid nineteenth century, these were frequently seen on English roadsides and the ones in use today have changed very little from the ones in use all those years ago. The Ledge, Burton and Reading Waggons, heavier to pull, expensive to buy and considerably more ornate, had their heyday at the turn of the century. The bow-top was and still is popular on the road, being relatively cheap and quick to build, easy for a horse to pull in hilly country and well designed for daily living and withstanding bad weather.

Built on a four-wheeled dray 9½-10 foot long and 5½-6 feet wide, the rear wheels are often larger than the front wheels. This gives a pleasing impression, adding grace and style to a truly beautiful home. Rising from the bed of the dray, a wooden raised ledge is built and to this the wooden bows or hoops are fixed, usually eight of them just over a foot apart. These originally were made of ash — soaked in water to ease the bending process and prevent snapping, but recently pirana pine has been used and with great success too. When these are in place, side planks are nailed the length of the waggon to provide a backrest when seated.

The crown boards at the front and the back top of each end provide solid stability, and then match-boarding at the front and back with doors and windows completes the whole structure. The whole of the bow top is then covered with a thick green duck-canvas, which is stretched taught, to keep out wind and water. Rain runs easily off a rounded roof, so chances of leakage are very slim. The canvas usually comes in three strips, which the sheet maker has pre-stitched to order. We have the seam edges facing the front so when the waggons are backed into the rain, water doesn't penetrate, but it's all a matter of preference. Wooden chamfered weatherboards are then put in place to secure the sheet further and to cover the sheet edges in a pleasing fashion. Chamfers are scallops carved out of the wood. As well as being very decorative, they make the waggon much lighter without compromising the strength of the wood.

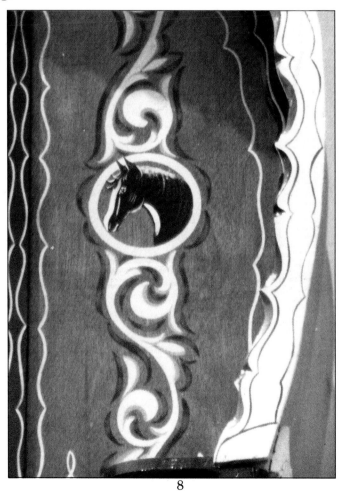

The front and back of the waggon is made of matchboard, "penny-farthing" boards being popular — so-called because they are the same width as an old penny and an old farthing side by side. The window at the back is either a three-sided bay window or a single pane with louvre shutters on either side. I like a bay window; a pair of frothy lace curtains really sets it off nicely. Below the window is a rack called a cratch, again over-sheeted with canvas, often used for horse food or hanging things off.

The waggon steps hang beneath it when travelling and a bale of hay or an old bike stored on it for journeys. When parked up, the harness is stored on it to keep it dry and well aired.

Below the cratch are more mysteries! A carved and decorated box with double doors — called a pan-box — is fixed at the rear of the waggon underneath the bed of the dray.

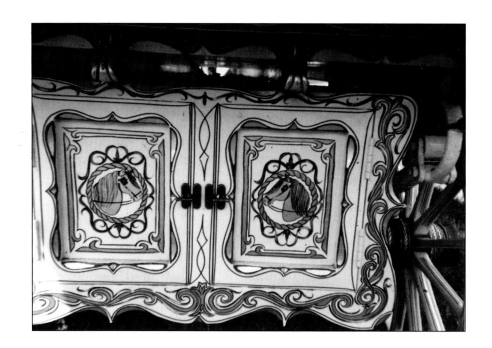

Although it's called a pan box and can be used as such, some families prefer to keep their "vittles" in it, it being a cool outside larder and handy as such when food is being prepared on an outside fire, little if any cooking taking place in the waggon itself. So that's the back.

Going round to the front, we have a pair of ash shafts, which the horse or cob goes between and these rest on turned wooden poles called shaft props. They prevent the shafts being damaged on the ground and come in very handy for hanging harness on or airing quilts and rugs!

The little metal wheel at the front on the step board turns a screwed rod to work the brake, which actions a block of wood to the rear wheels. This can be operated by one person driving from the step board, without needing to descend to the ground, so it's very convenient to apply.

The drag slide or drag shoe is also actioned on the rear wheels and is an extra fitting which hangs on the kerb side of the waggon fixed to the bed of the dray between the front and rear wheels. Here it is easily accessible in hilly country where the screw brake might be insufficient. The drag shoe is suspended on a chain and hooked up until a steep decline is reached, at which point it is unhooked and laid on the road for the rear wheel to roll onto. The rear wheel then no longer rolls and with traces taut, the horse often pulls the waggon down hill! It does make quite a loud rumbling noise on the tarmac as the iron plate scrapes along the ground and there's a tell-tale white line where the metal has scraped the roadway. Although the iron plate has wood above it to insulate the wheel, the drag shoe gets quite hot and needs cold water (or other available liquid) put on it if it starts to smoulder.

Another fitting rarely seen these days and worth a mention is a piece of equipment called a scotch roller which was fixed to the rear of the waggon's back wheel for up hill journeys. If the waggon had occasion to stop half way up the hill, it could be quite dangerous, the weight of a big waggon threatening to drag the horse back down with it. The roller prevented this happening by chocking the rear wheel immediately it started rolling backwards.

It was from the scotch roller that the term still used today "that's scotched 'em" was derived — meaning "that's stopped them".

The roller came into play much quicker than a wheel brake could be applied. I've known of hill accidents even today because rollers haven't been used. Perhaps a motorist has caused a waggon to stop mid-hill and the poor horse has lost its speed and impetus on the gradient and just can't get going again. The driver is perhaps struggling to keep to its head and can't get to the brake and that's it. Where a waggon is going up a bad hill with no rollers, it is always wise to have someone walk at the back with a block on a stick, or even a broom, just to chock that back wheel. If you've got a good *Vardo*, it's worth taking that extra time and the horse has a better chance of restarting the hill if it needs to.

Coming to the wheels now, wooden wheels with iron tyres are the best, noisiest, yes and again leaving the tell-tale white

lines in the road but much easier for a horse to pull. The noise from the iron bands drown out other noises that might startle the animal.

Wooden wheels on inlaid rubber tyres are another option, making travel much quieter and being kinder to the toes should one accidentally get run over! With the scarcity of wheelwrights these days, and the (often prohibitive) price of wooden wheels, seasoned oak being used for the spokes and fellies of ash and elm for the hub, alternatives are available. Artillery wheels — the type once seen on early motorcars — have metal spokes and inflated pump-up tyres. These do not roll as well as wooden wheels and do not have the variance in size or elegance but are still better than the "easy clean", "dustbin-lid" or car wheels, which are available for the modest pocket and I think quite ugly and tasteless!

Mounting the swan-necked steps now, we stand on the top one and see a brass carriage lamp at either side of the door. These are mounted on brass holders and are lit by candle with a spring device at the base, which automatically lifts the candle up to keep it in position as the wax melts down. They were often hidden out of sight when stationary so that lack of safe lighting could be given to *gavvers* (police) as an excuse not to be shifted! Many other excuses were also used, but this one *gavvers* took notice of because an unlit waggon travelling on the road at night was a danger to other road users.

Gypsy waggon doors always open outwards and showman's caravan doors always open inwards. Funny isn't it, that? Nobody really knows why, it's just the way it is. I did wonder if it was because there would be less room inside if they opened inwards but I don't actually know. Some waggons like the open-lots don't even have doors at all — just canvas sheeting hung onto hooks to keep out the weather and at night the two halves are laced together to keep the cold and rain out. Entering the waggon by opening the two halves of the top door and single lower door, we step inside. At the far end of the waggon there is a little bed that pulled out at night to double its size and pushed back during the day to take up less room.

Above it is a little window with a mist of lace curtains and a tiny shelf for photographs. Below this is the *chavvies'* bed, hidden from view by two cupboard doors, a secret and safe place to sleep. On the lefthand side of the waggon just through the door is a glass-fronted cabinet, the glass revealing lace-edged shelves where the finest china can be displayed.

This china cabinet might boast Crown Derby or Aynsley, very fine in quality and hand-decorated with real gold. The roof of the waggon is best lined with good carpet, giving extra insulation: cotton print can be used but isn't as warm nor does it stay in position so well. Next to the china cabinet will be the stove, most traditional being the Queenie or "Queen Anne Stove" — so named for the shape of the three legs that support its black cast-iron frame.

A chimney runs up to the roof while two hotplates on top of the stove provide cooking space for a kettle or stew pot should it be too wet for an outside fire. These hotplates are covered with a scrolled cover, highly ornamented, when not in use. The sliding doors can be parted for coal to be shovelled in or closed to make the stove draw better. A cast iron hearth houses an ashpan and drawplate. The entire stove is polished and shining using Zebo black lead polish — a graphite paste. Perhaps it's a sign of the times that I've recently been told Zebo in its yellow and black tube is no longer in production — not enough demand they say! I shall still be demanding it for a long time to come! Gypsies take great pride in a well-kept Queenie, tools of the trade being an old toothbrush to apply the polish and a soft rag to buff it off. I've talked a lot about these stoves, with their little figureheads, almost like imps and the fine detail. They're a joy to look at as well as being very efficient to warm a waggon all winter through. I'm told that like Zebo, Queenie stoves are no longer in production either, although some inferior copies are on sale at the fairs.

Next to the stove is a double seat: we have ours cushioned and upholstered in red velvet, making the seating more comfortable. Going round past the bed clockwise to the righthand side of the waggon, there is another single seat and then a table with a cupboard underneath. Often the tea-making things will be kept in here, sugar, biscuits, tea etc, and all the makings of an early morning cuppa.

Lace mats are on the table, of course, and then another seat, more or less opposite the stove and then a wardrobe cabinet, like the one for china, but with no glass in the door and pegs and a rail to hang clothes on. All the doors have tiny brass hinges and door catches and some waggons have lovely old-fashioned amber cut-glass handles. Beneath the seat ledges run lockers, which are hinged at the bottom and open downwards. These store polishes and cleaning materials, pegmaking tools, all the odds and ends kept tidy and out of sight yet close at hand.

In this miniature of homes every available inch of space is used to full advantage. A place for everything, and everything in its place. Folks always like to look inside a gypsy waggon and few get the chance. It's a miracle of shapes and colours and textures and styles, an Aladdin's cave of colour and light. No two are ever the same but the tried and tested layout varies very little. All wooden surfaces are grained or combed to create a uniform wood grain effect. Then each chamfer is picked out in colour — say red for example, then further lined out with white or cream. Some areas may be scrolled: free-hand scrolling is a curling-dancing pattern that flows across the surface, one brush stroke embracing the next — an art in itself.

Larger areas may be decorated with baskets of cascading fruit, grapes tumbling over ripe peaches and Victoria plums. The rococo style is reminiscent of that still seen in stately homes around the country! Elsewhere on lockers and drawers, horses' heads and horseshoes emerge from grapevines. Rearing coloured cobs, flying manes and tails, thick feathers, rope-work etc. All are original hand paintings, each with its own style.

The final touch, to protect the paintwork, a couple of coats of good quality yacht varnish. This brings together the many layers of paint and gives the work depth, rather like glass being put over a picture. The soft furnishings of satin, velvet and lace give a feeling of luxury and richness. Lace curtains at the windows and doors offered some privacy and velvet curtains give protection from the winter draughts.

Above the chimney pipe a valance of velvet and lace hides a tin plate set into the roof, which protects the canvas above from heat damage. The carpeted floor has rugs for extra warmth and set off a painted stool, perhaps for extra seating and a coal bucket and tongs to replenish the Queenie stove.

The outside of the waggon: the underworks are usually primrose, yellow or cream. This is then picked out decoratively with red or green chamfers whilst the body of the waggon will be maroon or maybe red or green, traditional colours, the fashion for which never seems to change. Below the front of the waggon is the lock, which holds the circular greased metal turntable. The ends of the lock are carved like fiddle heads — the tuning part of violins. Between the wheels are the axle-cases, which a wood turner has turned to give a circular and ribbed finish.

Some waggons have a wooden cage on the outside at the front. *Gorgios* think these are for chickens but instead halters and horse stuff is best kept there so the driver can easily access them without leaving go of the reins. The chimney has a cowl on top to help prevent rain from running down the chimney. The ledgeboards above the wheels have decorated panels, again with scrolls, fruit or horses.

The front of the waggon has two ledge seats, which can hold the driver should he wish to ride-up or hold the water jacks (cans) when the waggon is not on the road. There are two corresponding ledges at the back, also useful for storage. This completes our tour of the bow-top vardo both inside and out.

There is more than one type of Gypsy Waggon. From the pack ponies and donkeys came the pony and cart, from the pony and cart came the accommodation top (or whoopy) and then the open-lot, the simplest of waggons, easiest to construct and maintain with a canvas bow-top, and two canvas sheets in place of a door.

These can be laced up at night or during bad weather and tied back or removed during the day. The bow-top we have looked at in detail.

An interesting variation is the square-bow, shaped as its name describes. This allows more headroom and space to stand and it is possible to add windows to the sides if desired.

The Ledge waggon has a narrower floor space and an over-hang for the sides. The top has a solid roof with a raised mollycroft running lengthways down the centre. This allowed glass panes to be used for windows in the roof.

The Reading Waggon is the most luxurious type of caravan, gaining its name from the place in Berkshire where many were built. They are sometimes called a Dunton Van, after the firm that built them. They are made entirely of wood with the sides match-boarded. Large rear wheels and porch brackets handsomely carved are both hallmarks of this waggon. They are mainly seen only in museums or occasionally at Gypsy fairs. Some fine examples are in private collections and do from time to time pass through the carriage auctions in Reading itself.

The Reading Waggon was best suited to flat country because being of heavier construction it usually needed two horses to pull it. It has a window at each side and sliding shutters. A truly ornate vehicle, its heyday was the 1900s and only wealthy Gypsies owned one!

The Burton Waggon, also called a Showman's had an inwards-opening door and less ostentatious decoration.

Finally the Brush or Fen Waggon — the outward appearance being like a travelling shop. Racks were made to display brushes, brooms and wicker chairs that the family sold as they moved from place to place. Examples of the Brush Waggon are very rare.

This concludes the introduction to Gypsy Waggons. There is so much more to discover I hope this has awakened your interest.

On the Move Again

When you live in a horse drawn Gypsy waggon or bow-top, you're on the move quite often, every time the horses have run out of grass to eat! Stopping places — what *gorgios* would call camping grounds — are few and far between because to make them good stopping places, they need quite a few things.

Firstly there needs to be plenty of grass, as horses eat a lot. Secondly there needs to be shelter. Waggons can blow over in a high wind and horses need some protection too — in winter from the storms and in summer from the sun. Nobody wants to stop too near busy roads, as traffic can be a hazard especially where there are children and animals about. Then there's water. It's handy to be near a stream or brook for horses' water — they drink gallons every day, and fresh drinking water has to be fetched in daily in churns, either begged or borrowed if need be. We get through a lot of *cosh* too. An outside *yog* is a pleasure as well as a necessity and a curl of blue woodsmoke is a pleasing sight to come home to, in the dusk of an evening.

So that's the sort of place we look for when we want to move and of course we need to be near to a few shops and people so we can earn a bit of a living as well. Don't want much really do we!

On a day when we're shifting, things start early. First up lights the *yog* and checks none of the *grys* have done a runner in the night. They should be tethered out nearby either grazing or stood with their backs to the wind — resting one leg, in the way cobs do best.

After a cup of *meskie*, or two, or three, there's sometimes a quick breakfast, sometimes not. Then the women and girls 'pack-down' and the men and boys 'yoke-up'. Packing-down the waggon means putting all the china and breakables away safely so nothing gets broken on the journey. Over rough ground or at the trot, gear gets rattled around a lot, so packing down properly and quickly is an important job. Windows and doors need to be secured so they're not flying open either. Outside, the men will be bringing the *gry* up and running a brush over it's back to tidy it up — if there's time. There will be the tether-chain and pin to stow on the cratch and the harness, and straps to put on.

An experienced cob will stand patiently and untied while all this goes on, quite unperturbed by all the extra activity. A younger animal might not be so helpful and sensing the impending move gets over-excited and won't want to stand well at all. A few miles under the collar and they settle down — usually! The outside *yog* will be stamped out and any remaining possessions stowed on the cratch at the back of the waggon. Steps will be hung from or put on the cratch and if there's a *jukle* (dog) that might be tied to the back as well — frowned upon by authorities but kinder to the animal than getting run over by a car. When all is ready, the horse will be 'yoked-up!' It's easier with two people, but a good waggon-horse can be handled alone. The horse will gently be backed between the wooden shafts and then the traces hooked on and the breeching straps buckled up. When this is complete and the harness correct, the *gry* will be ready to pull off. We usually walk at their heads for a short way just to settle them down, then ride up and drive them (from the kerbside of the waggon). Horses have four legs and we have two, so walking at their heads for any distance is a bit of a mug's game — unless you just happen to like walking.

At a gentle pace, we maybe do three miles an hour, but can go faster if needed, trotting probably for half of the journey time. There's a lot of *dinelos* on the roads who don't like to get stuck behind us doing three miles an hour and on a busy road there's soon a big tailback, so we like to be on the road early before it's too busy if it's a main road, and then on the quiet back roads as soon as we can. There's truly nothing nicer than driving a good cob in a pretty waggon down a country lane. I never do tire of it. When we get to wherever we're going, we try and find a flat piece of ground to pull on. The *gry* stands quietly while the straps are undone and then it's walked out of the shafts and unharnessed. I can't emphasize enough: a good horse is worth double it's weight in gold and makes life so much easier. Once out of the harness, it'll be rubbed down and then plugged-out so it can have a roll on the

ground maybe, then have a well-earned rest and get its head down for a feed. Hedgerow grass isn't horse-sick like paddock grass so often is and has a fine mix of grasses and herbs, which are a healthier diet supplemented by the berries and leaves of the hedge itself.

On the way back to the waggon, a few dry sticks will be pulled out of the hedge and the men will light an outside fire and put the kettle on — for more cups of tea. The collar will be put to dry and the harness maybe put on the cratch. By this time the women will have unpacked the waggon and put everything out in its place again. Then out comes the hoop-handled frying pan or the stew pan and it's time for a late breakfast or an early tea. We have successully moved again!

Glossary of Romany Words

chavvies	children
cosh	sticks for firewood
dineloes	idiots
gavvers	policemen
gorgios	non-gypsies
grys	horses
jukle	dog
rye	gentleman
meskie	tea
vardo	Gypsy waggon
victuals	(vittles) old word for food
yog	fire